Brogg's
Brain

Also by the Author
THE APE INSIDE ME

Kin Platt

Brogg's Brain

J. B. LIPPINCOTT   NEW YORK

Library of Congress Cataloging in Publication Data

Platt, Kin.
Brogg's brain.
SUMMARY: Everyone is convinced that all Monty needs to be the fastest miler
on the high school track team is heart. Monty himself is not so sure he's got
what it takes until he sees a movie called "Brogg's Brain."
    [1. Running—Fiction]   I. Title.
PZ7.P7125Br   1981   [Fic]   79–9622
                                                AACR2
ISBN 0–397–31945–2   ISBN 0–397–31946–0 (lib. bdg.)

1 2 3 4 5 6 7 8 9 10

First Edition

1

I was out on the track doing my laps. It was a hot day. There was the smell of smog in the air and I was dragging. One more lap, I told myself. Just do it and go on in. You don't have to kill yourself.

I guess it was one of the slowest miles I ever ran. But I'm not that terrific anyway, so it didn't bother me. When I finished, Coach Gordon whistled me over. He didn't look happy.

"Davis," he said, "you were dragging your butt

out there. You're supposed to be running that mile, not walking it."

I waved a hand at the air. "It's hot out, Coach."

He nodded. "It might be even hotter at the dual meet. You're supposed to run, not worry about the conditions."

"Right on, Coach," I said. "I'll do better tomorrow."

"Tomorrow?" he barked. "We're still working on today." He looked down at his clipboard. Found my name and chart. "Let's do some intervals. Not all out. Just so you put in the work."

I looked out at the track. A couple of our guys were still on it, pounding away. Heat waves were shimmering off the grass around the oval.

"Intervals," I said. Intervals were like repetitions. You did the same thing over and over. They meant work. I looked down at my running shoes. They felt hot and soggy. Same as me.

"Right," Coach said. He began scribbling on the paper chart. "Start with some four-hundreds at three-quarter speed."

"How many?" It was a dumb question because I know Coach likes to see a lot.

He grinned. "Say five. And some three-hundreds at the same pace. Do three of them. Then do about five one-hundreds to build up some speed."

"That all?" I said. Another dumb question.

He shook his head. "Finish up with a slow mile or two, if you can handle it. Just a warmdown."

I didn't argue. At Emerson High, you don't talk back to the teachers or coaches. They're only doing their job.

I looked out at the steaming track again. "Hey, Coach, what if I drop dead out there? It's really hot, you know."

"No problem, Davis," he said. "If you drop dead, you get a break. You get tomorrow off."

2

My old man is kind of a jock. He likes all sports. According to him, he was a top sprinter back in his school days. He didn't keep his medals, he told me. So I have to take his word for it. He has a pot belly now, and heavy legs.

I got home late after track, still dragging. They were about to start dinner. He got up, clapped me on the back.

"Well, Monty, how did it go today? Put in your laps?"

I dropped my gym bag. "Too many. It was hot out there, pop. I was really dragging."

He clapped his hands together and rubbed them briskly. "That's the time to pour it on, son. When it's bad outside is when you get tough inside. When's that dual meet?"

"Two weeks."

"Good," he said. "You'll be ready for it."

"Yeah, if I don't die first," I said.

He laughed and waved me off. "Not a chance." He thumped his chest. "You've got a heart like your old man. You'll run those other kids into the ground."

I headed for the bathroom. "Well, don't count on it," I said over my shoulder. "It's only a little meet, you know. Between us and Culver High. Not worth dying over."

Mom came out of the kitchen. She looked worried. "What were you saying about dying?"

I shook my head. "Just kidding, mom. Pop's got the idea I'm the greatest miler around. I'm just kind of preparing him for the agony of defeat."

She put a wet hand on my cheek. "Well, nobody ordered you to go out for the track team. It was your own idea."

I bobbed my head. "I know. That's one of the problems with being a kid and not knowing too much about your parents."

5

She stepped back. "Why, Monty, what do you mean?"

I shrugged. "Maybe insanity runs in the family," I said. "Maybe I'm crazy going out for the mile. Probably only about a hundred kids in L.A. are faster than me."

She looked at me. "Well, that's one thing you're going to find out, then. Isn't it?"

"More or less," I said, stepping into the bathroom. I closed the door and looked at myself in the mirror. "Who's the greatest miler in L.A.?" I said to the mirror. It didn't answer, naturally. "That's okay," I told it. "Take your time."

3

My kid sister Judy came back from the library. She was carrying about ten books. It's a long walk from the library even without ten books, and she looked beat.

"How come so many books?" I said.

"How come? Because it's such a dumb library," she said. "It's the dumbest library I ever saw. It never has any of the books I want."

I pointed to the stack she had. "Well, you did all right, it looks like."

7

Judy's twelve and has a hot temper. She lashed out with her hand and scattered the big pile of books all over the table. "Sure I got a lot of books. But none of them are the ones I really wanted. I just took them because I didn't have anything to read."

I picked up one and looked at the title. "*Mountain Climbing in Tibet?* Why do you want to know about climbing mountains?"

She shook her head. "I don't. I wanted something about surfing. This was all they had left on sports. That's what I mean about it being a dumb library. Who cares about mountains in Tibet?"

I had to laugh. "Far out," I said.

As I was turning away, she said, "Hey, Monty, are you going to win your mile in that big meet?"

I stopped. "How do I know if I'll win? Ask me after it's over. Maybe then I'll know for sure."

She nodded. "I have a friend whose brother goes to Culver. They have some pretty good milers, she says."

"Okay," I said. "Good for them."

She frowned. "So you have to train harder to beat them, don't you?"

I shrugged. "I'm training. Doing my workouts. If the guys they got are better than me, they'll win, won't they?"

"Not if you train harder," she said. "I heard pop

say if you trained harder, you could beat anybody."

"Well, that's his opinion," I said. "I just like to run. I don't see where I have to knock myself out to beat everybody."

She grinned. "What does your coach say about that."

"Do more laps, is what he says. He'd be happy if I ran a hundred miles a week."

"Maybe he's right. He ought to know about that stuff."

"Maybe," I said. "Only I'm not doing it. This isn't the Olympics, you know. It's just a ratty little track meet."

"Well," she said, "even so. You want to win, don't you?"

I stared at her. "I just want to run in it. If I win, okay. If I don't, that's okay, too."

She stared right back. "You're weird," she said.

"I guess so," I said, "but I didn't pick the book on mountain climbing in Tibet."

"Pop won't like it," she said darkly. "He'll think you let him down."

"So what?" I said. "Say, whose life is this anyway?"

I walked out of her room then. Wondering if I was weird, after all.

4

I did my homework after dinner. Math, History, English. There was a book report due soon for my English class. I wondered if maybe I should do it on climbing mountains in Tibet.

Judy looked up from her small white study desk. "You want to borrow what?"

I picked it out of the pile. "I need to do a book report. Maybe I'll read this."

She rolled her eyes. "Mountain climbing? Why don't you stick to something you know? Like track."

"Track is just going around in a circle." I tapped the book cover. "In this stuff, you go up and down. Sounds like more fun."

She bent over her notebook again. "Suit yourself. I also took out one on poetry, if you want it. Maybe it will come in handy when you want to write some love letters."

"I'll get to that after I climb my mountain," I said. I took her book back to my room and sat down with it. But I was too pumped up, too restless. Before I knew what I was doing, I was into my running gear, lacing up my shoes.

Pop saw me about to go out. His face creased into a big smile. "That's my boy," he said proudly. "I knew you'd be going all out for this one."

"Take it easy, pop," I said. "I'm just going to jog around the park. No big deal."

He raised his fist. "Way to go, son." He tapped his belly and got a drum sound. "If I wasn't carrying all this beef, I'd join you. Running used to be my life, you know. Never found anything I liked as much."

"How about mountain climbing?"

He looked puzzled. "Huh?"

I waved and went out the door. "See you."

Poor pop, I thought. He's dying for that medal, and I couldn't care less. As I jogged down to the

11

park, I was trying to get my head together. What was happening? I was only fifteen, but it seemed as if I had a contract with everybody to win.

No sweat, I told myself. You'll win if you're good enough.

That sounded too easy. Maybe because it made simple sense. But the way things were going, it was as if I had to explain to everybody this simple little thing. You win if you're good enough.

They had other ideas. If you train hard, if you go all out, if you want to win, you'll win. Winning is the only thing. Nothing else matters.

The park is a half-mile from our house. It has three diamonds laid out for softball, slowball, and hardball. A good soccer field. A picnic area, rec center, and swimming pool. Swings, seesaws and sand pits for the little kids.

The trail around the outside edge is almost a mile long. Eight-tenths. Around twice is 1.6, three times is 2.4, five times is 4 miles, and so on. It's long enough so that you don't get dizzy or bored going around and around.

It was still light and I felt wound up enough to do a few miles easily. There wasn't any point in timing myself. It was just an evening workout to let off some steam. Anyway, I've been running for so long, I have a pretty good idea from my pace what time I'm doing. And there's a big difference between running easy and going all out for time.

I went around twice at about three-quarter speed, and needed more. Five times around, for the four miles, ought to do it, I thought. Nobody to beat— just me and the park and my running shoes. The good feeling of your body going well for you. Like a magical machine, well oiled, running good.

There were other joggers going around the narrow trail—some older people trying to stay in shape, some maybe in training for the big marathon, some not meant to be runners, but going at it anyway with short steps and red faces. There are all kinds of runners.

On the north side of the rectangular course, the path runs through the woods. Soft turf, trees, a lot of shade picking you up each time you go around.

I saw red running pants flashing ahead of me, a blond ponytail bobbing. White top, red shoes. A girl with a long stride, going at a good fast pace. I revved up my system and moved faster to close the gap between us.

She was a hundred yards ahead of me. The straightaway through the woods was about four hundred yards long. I picked up my pace, but the pony-tail still bobbed tantalizingly ahead of me. A good steady runner, I thought. She's put her miles in.

13

With two hundred yards to go, I had closed the gap between us to about thirty yards. She must have sensed me gaining on her because now she was putting distance between us again. The ponytail was dancing from side to side. I didn't know any more about her than one thing: she wasn't going to let anybody pass her on this long stretch.

Let's see, I told myself, and began sprinting, going all out. She heard me coming up hard and increased her own drive. I was just slightly behind her, with about fifty yards to go. The park trail narrows at that point and runners must go single file to avoid the bushes and trees that border the path on both sides, especially one big tree near the end.

We were running abreast now, side to side, shoulder to shoulder, going all out. I was pulling slightly ahead with ten yards to go. Directly in front of us was the big tree. One of us had to pass the other clean or run into it.

I looked quickly at her face. It was set hard, her teeth gritted, her eyes straight ahead. Her arms and legs were driving like pistons, her fists clenched. No way was she going to ease up and let me by.

I could have done it, surged ahead of her with a step or two to spare. Making her break stride, fall behind. It was happening awfully fast, and I could hear my heart pounding along with my feet.

I took another quick look. She knew I was there. She was going to beat me to that tree, or else.

All of a sudden, it didn't seem that important. I eased up, fell back. She flashed ahead, digging hard into the ground, leaning forward as if she had the finish-line tape to break.

When I got to the end of the park, she had stopped and was doing some stretches. I slowed to a walk and came up to her. She seemed to be about my age, or maybe a year older.

"Good run," I said.

She stared at me with unsmiling light blue eyes. "Why did you quit?" she said. "Because I'm a girl?"

I shrugged. "I don't know. That tree was bigger than both of us."

She stood flexing her body, her hands on her hips. "I knew it was there. Don't you like to fight for things?"

It was my turn to try the stare. "Maybe," I said. "Only they have to be important."

I turned away and jogged off. There were still a few miles left to do on my earlier plan. But suddenly all the fun had gone out of it.

I walked home.

5

The next day our tenth-grade English teacher, Mr. Robinson, asked the class what books we'd chosen for our reports. He's a young, pretty loose guy, and sometimes we share some laughs in class.

A few of the girls were into books on finding themselves, on becoming their own kind of people. That sounded like something I was interested in myself.

Mr. Robinson was especially pleased with that group. "I'm interested in that kind of awareness for you kids," he said. "In my day, nobody thought about it. As a result, when we grew up it was almost too late to find out who we were."

Our class joker, Barry Sproat, had something to say about that. "If you don't know who you are, how can you be sure it's you when you find out?"

Mr. Robinson let the class laugh over that for a bit. "Some people can identify themselves easily enough, once they read a good book on the subject. In your case, Sproat, you might have to read two books."

Barry groaned. Everybody laughed and hooted and began coming at him.

"He's too gross even for two books. Barry needs a dozen."

"If it's about people, Barry can forget it. He needs one on animals."

"He'll never find himself in a book. Maybe somewhere out in space."

When it got to be too much, Mr. Robinson called for some other ideas. When he called on me, I was ready. "It's on mountain climbing." The class started buzzing again.

He looked at me, cocking his head. "Mountain climbing? Is that your hobby, Davis?"

"No, I just thought it might be interesting to try a book on something I don't know anything about. My kid sister had the book."

He nodded, interested. "A sound reason, and a good idea for a report. For some of you who haven't made up your minds yet, I'd be happy if you followed Monty Davis's lead. Get your heads into something new, something that might grab your attention." He sighed, looking beat. "You don't know how boring it is to get the same reports on the same books over and over again, year after year."

He got them talking and asking questions. Before the bell, a lot of the kids were high on new things, topics that came up in the general loose discussion we'd had.

Marine biology. Archaeology. Anthropology. Underwater photography. Computer technology. Geophysics. Electronics.

Mr. Robinson held up his hand. "This has been a very gratifying day," he said. "I haven't heard a movie or rock star mentioned once. And to prove how interested I am, I promise to raise anybody's mark by ten points for new ideas."

The class went a little crazy about that, too, and then the bell rang and it was time to go. Mr. Robinson waved me over to his desk. I wondered why.

"How's it going on the track team?" he asked.

"Okay, I guess," I said.

"What's your event?"

"Mile. I'm not fast enough for the eight-eighty."

He smiled. "I ran the mile myself back in school," he said.

Here it comes, I thought, another hotshot like my old man. "Were you any good?" I said, "Or just average?"

He sighed. "I was very good. I was too good, actually."

I looked at him. "How come?"

He shrugged. "You don't have to take my word for it. It's still in the record books. I was one of the first in high school to break four minutes for the mile." I stared. "You'll find it under state championships. John F. Robinson. Segundo High. That was 1960. New state and meet record."

My jaw dropped. Hardly any high school runners come close to a four-minute mile. Not many college guys do, either. And here was my English teacher telling me he ran *under* four minutes?

I looked him over. He was average in size, nothing special. But good milers come in all sizes. Jim Ryun was tall. Sebastian Coe is small. Steve Ovett is in between. All champions.

Mr. Robinson was reading my mind. "Jim Ryun was the first schoolboy to break four minutes. Then came Marty Liquori. I was among the next few who did it."

I shook my head, still in awe about it. "I couldn't

break four minutes if I had somebody after me with a gun."

He grinned. "You never know. One thing for sure, it would help you pick up your time."

I shrugged. "I die anyway, even at four-twenty."

He nodded. "You always die," he said. "It doesn't matter what time you do, if you're doing your best, going all out, you die. Perhaps I had a better threshold of pain than most. Or it was more important to me to run through it."

"I guess you must have had a good coach," I said.

He rubbed his jaw. "I thought so, at the time. When I was the school hero. Winning all the track meets. Later, I wasn't so sure."

"How come?"

"I was burned out. By the time I got to college, there wasn't anything left. Not another four-minute mile. Nothing even close. It happens. You never think it will happen to you. Later on, I thought maybe my coach should have known better. But he wanted it all then, just like me."

"You must have been fast naturally," I said. "To begin with. I just like running. I know I can't be the best. So I don't have that problem."

He grinned again. "Maybe not. But I can bet you have another. I know Coach Gordon. Like other coaches, he likes his boys to win."

"Yeah, well, sure," I said.

He looked at me slyly. "Perhaps others, too, right? Want you to put out more?"

I sighed. "You guessed it. In fact, everybody I can think of wants me to win more than I do myself."

He laughed. We had walked out of the classroom. He closed the door and locked it. Then he looked me over, nodding his head. "That's no problem. All it takes is a certain amount of courage."

I waved my hand. "Well, that stuff about feeling that I'm dying when I run hard. I don't really mind it that much. Sometimes I think I even like it."

He shook his head. "Enduring is only instinct. Courage is something else. Not as exciting. Sometimes it has its own rewards."

I looked at him, puzzled.

He shifted some books under his arm. "I'm talking about the courage to dare to be unpopular. To please only yourself. To do what only *you* want to do."

I thought about it. Finally I shook my head. "I don't think Coach Gordon would go for that." I couldn't see my old man being happy about it, either.

Mr. Robinson turned his hands over, palms up. "Neither will anybody else. I thought we were talking about *you*."

I stared at him.

"Think it over," he said, and walked off.

After school, I was working out along with the rest of the track team. Big Jake Jarvis, our big shot-putter, was spinning himself around on the infield throwing his monster twelve-pound steel ball. He'd throw it, walk out about fifty feet and pick it up, then walk back and throw it again. Our jumpers were loosening up, doing leg and body work and stretches.

Coach Gordon was with our two best milers, Jerry Cott and Don Rose. They're seniors, both faster and stronger than I am. Our school has always had a good track team. Maybe it's because we've never been so hot at basketball or football, and we had to win at something. Or maybe it was due to Coach Gordon and his drills, the tough workouts he puts you through over and over again.

I had done my stretches, and was jogging along, still warming up. I saw Cott and Rose lining up on the track, as if they were going to race. Coach had his stopwatch in his hand. He probably wanted to time them again at their top speed before our dual meet. He raised his arm, and, as he clicked his timer, yelled "Go!" Both runners took off, Cott on the inside.

I was near the first short turn, about ten yards ahead of them. When they took off, I turned around and did the same. I'd never raced against Cott and Rose before. They're too good. But I'd always wondered how I would do in a race with them, how much they would beat me by. So I let out as if it was going to be a real race.

The first lap was fast, my fastest ever. I didn't want them to lap me right from the start. I heard them pounding behind me, but I took a quick look over my shoulder on the long straightaway and they weren't gaining, either. Okay, I told myself, hang in there. Make them work for it.

When I passed Coach the first time around, he

was staring at me and yelling something. I didn't hear what he said, but he looked mad, and I guessed he wanted me out of there. Don't worry, I told him silently, I'm just a rabbit for those two hotshots. When they're ready to pass, I'll move over.

A rabbit in track is the guy who shoots out ahead and sets a fast pace. He isn't expected to win and, as a rule, has to drop out. The idea is to make the other guys pick up their speed and maybe set a new record. I'd never been one before. So far, it was fun.

I figured if I went all out I could hold them off for three laps of the four anyway before I folded. But by the end of the second lap, when I looked back, I had picked up another five yards on them. Also, I wasn't feeling much pain, and had a lot left inside.

It was the fastest 880 I'd ever run. I didn't have my watch on but I knew. Also Cott and Rose were very good. If they weren't on my heels yet, I had to be doing something right.

Into the third lap, I poured on some more speed. My stride was good. I was running very easily. Nice and smooth, the way you want to do it. At the far stretch, I sneaked another look. I couldn't believe it. I had put even more distance between us, almost twenty yards now. It was crazy.

But Cott and Rose were too good to take my dust. Near the end of the third lap, they started to come at me around the last short turn. Cott was leading Rose by a yard or so, his arms and legs driving hard.

Well, here we go, I thought. I knew Cott's best time for the mile. It was the best in the city. Around 4:10. Rose had done a few 4:12s. This was the bell lap, the gun lap, the key to the whole mile. They both had good strong finishing kicks. And I was the rabbit they were going to eat alive. Along with that thought came the pain.

I was feeling it now, going into the last lap. And I must have eased up because at the first short turn, they were close behind me. I could hear hard breathing over my shoulder. Somebody else was breathing hard, too, and it sounded like me. My chest was on fire. I needed air.

It's okay, I told myself. Run through it.

You tell yourself that, or you'd never finish.

I could imagine this was how it was going to be in the dual meet coming up. If I got a good lead, I'd lose it. It wouldn't matter where we stood in the race. Somehow by the time it was over, I'd find a way to lose it.

The pain got worse on the far straightaway. My chest hurt really bad, and my legs were starting to cramp up. Oh, come on, I told myself. This isn't a real race. It's for fun. Let's do well for a change. It doesn't matter now if you win or lose. Let's show those guys.

They were still close at the far turn. Cott was stepping out for his big kick. There was no way I'd be able to keep up with him then. I needed a bigger lead right now. I leaned into the turn and everything fell into place. I forgot the pain.

I've lost races before by looking over one shoulder while some guy passed me on the other. No peeking, just run, I told myself. *Come on, drive!*

Cott's footsteps were coming closer. Then he was on my shoulder, angling to cut in. But I shouldered him off and found some more speed somewhere. I went down the final stretch still leading, trying not to fall. I saw Coach raise his clocking hand. Hold on, I told myself, don't die on me.

There wasn't any tape, but there was a finish line. I was past it by two steps before I came apart. Cott and Rose went by me, seconds apart. I was bent over, gasping, trying not to be sick, when I felt a hand on my shoulder.

It was Coach. His face was red, his voice high and excited. "What got into you, Davis?" he yelled.

I shrugged, trying to get my wind back. Cott and Rose were walking toward us. Neither one looked happy. I gestured to them. "Just figured I'd be a rabbit for those guys, Coach. Give them something to go after."

He was shaking his head. His big hands were balled into fists, jamming his hips. "You know what time you did?"

I waved my hand. "Don't tell me. Anyway, I had about ten yards on Cott and Rose, Coach. So it doesn't count."

He looked at his watch. Then back at me. "You had fifteen after two laps. Five yards at the finish. It counts, all right."

Cott and Rose came by. Cott waved his hand. "Hey, Monty, was that really you out there?"

"It couldn't have been," Rose said. "This guy wouldn't quit."

I had to smile. "Remember, I had a big lead," I said.

Cott nodded his head. "Yeah, from start to finish."

"Maybe he's taking dope," Rose said. "Think we ought to have him tested?"

Coach stepped in. Waved his hand. "Okay, you two hotshots. Take a couple more laps. If Davis can beat you, we're all in trouble."

They took off, jogging easily. Coach was frowning, putting numbers down on his charts. "That was a neat trick," he said, finally.

"How do you mean, Coach?" I said.

27

"All this time you had me faked out," he said. "Always one excuse or another. You're not fast enough. You're too beat. You feel weak. It's always too hot for your run."

"Well, it's true," I said. "Anyway, this wasn't a real race. Those two guys can take me easily."

Coach waved his hand. The watch was in it. "Maybe," he said. "Maybe the race wasn't real. But the time is."

I felt sick. "Maybe you got it wrong, Coach," I said.

He shook his head. Still looking mad. "It says four-ten, Davis. You know what that means?"

I had a feeling I didn't want to know. I looked at him dumbly. "No, sir," I said.

"It means," he said. "you can't fake me out any longer."

"But Coach—" I said.

He put the watch in front of my eyes. "The watch doesn't lie, Davis. From now on, I've got to rate you with the best milers we've got."

"Oh, come on, Coach," I said. "It was an accident. I'll never come near that time again."

He was nodding his head, grinning fiercely. "Oh, yes you will. You can bet on it."

"How come?" I said.

"Because I'll be working you out harder from now on," he said. He pointed out to the track. "Now get out there and do four more laps."

I did that. Not breaking any records this time.

7

Cindy Watanabe was walking briskly ahead of me. Her long straight black hair was shining, as usual. I like Cindy and think sometimes she likes me. But I'm never sure. She's Japanese-American, third generation here in L.A. Her grandfather came over in 1898. I know about Hiroshima and Nagasaki, where we dropped the big A-bombs, killing an awful lot of innocent people. Also about how we rounded up all the Japanese people who were living here, took away their property, and sent them off to live in prison camps in the desert. I always have the feeling Cindy holds this against me. It could be all in my mind, as she is always friendly with me. Maybe I'm just carrying the guilt.

She turned, saw me, stopped, and waited. When I reached her, she gave me her cool smile and added her very soft voice. "Hi, Monty. Where have you been? I don't see you around much lately."

"I'm trying to keep it a secret, Cindy, but I'll let you in on it," I said. "I went out for the track team. So now I'm spending all my free time running and sweating."

"Oh?" she said. "What event are you in?"

"The mile," I said. "There's Jerry Cott, Don Rose, and myself. They're the big guns. I'm only hacking it."

She nodded, picked up her walk, and took me along. "What times do you do?"

I looked at her. I still didn't believe what had happened at practice. "Around four-twenty," I said.

She laughed. "That's just about what I do."

I stopped. "Are you for real? You do four-twenty for the mile?"

She shook her head. Her long hair bounced. "Not the mile. The marathon."

I stared. The marathon is a little over twenty-six miles. What I do in minutes, Cindy does in hours.

But twenty-six miles! Plus 385 yards!

"How can you run a marathon?" I said. "I don't know if I'd live that long."

"Oh, it's not so bad," she said. "You just have to train yourself to suffer."

I clapped my head. "I can suffer just thinking about it."

She laughed again. "Maybe we can run together sometime," she said. "Talking when you run builds up your wind."

"Gee, Cindy, I don't know if I can talk for four hours."

"No problem," she said laughing. "That was my worst time. I'm cutting it down to three and a half hours now. At least that's my new goal, and I'm getting close. Can you talk for three and a half hours?"

"I guess so," I said. "But I'm training to be a miler. I don't know if running marathons would be good for me. Even if I could run that far, which I doubt."

"Well, try it and see," she said.

"I'll have to think about it," I said. "I don't know if my old man would like me running long distance now. I'm supposed to be training for the dual meet with Culver High."

"What's your father got to do with it?" she said.

I shrugged. "He used to be some kind of a hotshot sprinter when he was in school. Or so he tells me.

And he likes to pass on his know-how to me."

"Really?" Cindy said. "That's kind of weird."

"Oh, I don't know," I said. "He gets a big kick out of it. Like he's living his track life all over again with me."

"I understand," Cindy said. "I didn't mean it was weird, him doing that. I can understand that."

"You didn't?" I said. "I mean, you can?"

She bobbed her head. "Of course. The weird part is you."

I must have looked puzzled. "Me? How come?"

She smiled and touched my arm. "Your father had his life. This one is yours."

I wasn't able to come up with an answer to that. Then Cindy's bus came along, and she went for it. I had the long walk back to my house to think over what she had said.

By the time I got there, I knew she was right. Okay, she's right, I told myself. What can you do about it?

I couldn't come up with an answer to that, either.

8

I decided it wouldn't be a good idea to tell my old man what had happened at track practice. If he heard that I'd held off Rose and Cott for the mile in good time, he'd be on my back every minute. We don't go into detail about everything in my training, but he's always on me, asking how I'm doing, and so on. Anyway, I still considered my terrific run an accident. So that evening when he asked me how I did, I said okay, and let it go at that.

"Okay isn't bad," he said. "But with that dual meet coming up after next week, you ought to be clocking some good times now. Crank it up, Monty. You can always do better, you know. That's what the training program is for."

"Yeah, well, Coach isn't worried," I said. "He'll get enough points with Cott and Rose. Plus we can pick up some in the four-forty and high jump. We've got one guy breaking fifty, and the other kid is jumping six two without taking off his warmup pants."

"What about the hundred and the two-twenty?" he asked. "Don't you have any sprinters?"

"We've got a couple, pop, but nobody real fast."

He smacked a fist into his open hand. "In my day everybody was fast. I had to work my tail off to beat them out. That's the trouble with you kids today. You're all taking it easy, riding in cars."

"Don't forget roller skating," I said.

He gave me a disgusted look. "Yeah, that, too. And I don't see anybody going all out for speed on those fancy wheels, either. They're all just oozing along, just taking a ride."

"Well, that's what it's for, pop," I said. "It took over from the skateboards."

He held up his hand to stop me. "Let's not even talk about that. Just a bunch of hotshots showing off."

"Well, what did you do for fun when you were a kid?"

His jaw jutted and his eyes glared hard at me. "I trained—we all did. Ran and ran and ran. That's what we did for fun. We worked for it."

Judy happened to be passing through the room and caught some of this. "You sound like you were all crazy. What's wrong with fun?"

Pop had a glare left for Judy, too. "Fun is fine," he said. "Just so you do the important things first."

"Big deal," Judy said. "I don't see that it did you all that much good. You're thirty pounds overweight, and your knees are in such bad shape you can't even play tennis. Maybe you overdid, pop."

He snapped out his newspaper. "Maybe. But I didn't baby my body. It's better to wear out than to rust out."

Judy looked at me. "Remember that, Monty. I've got enough on my mind."

"Don't get smart, young lady," he said. "Besides, I wasn't addressing this to you. I was talking to your brother, trying to light a fire under him. He doesn't seem to realize we've got a dual meet coming up with Culver High."

"You mean, *he's* got, pop. It's his school against theirs. If Monty isn't worried about it, well, that's his problem, isn't it?"

Pop got very red in the face. I could tell he didn't want to be closed out of this. "Monty can talk for himself. You know you can always tell me when I'm pressing you too hard, right, son?"

I looked at him. He really believed it. "Sure, pop," I said. "No sweat, it's okay."

Judy gave me a disgusted look. Her lip curled. I couldn't blame her. Here she was, sticking up for me, and I'd jumped right back in the hole.

Chicken, I guess.

Most nights I sleep like a log. This time I didn't. I got up earlier than usual. The sun wasn't in sight yet. Before I knew what I was doing, I was into my running shoes. Might as well do a few miles before breakfast, I told myself.

Pop was at the table finishing breakfast. He saw me and beamed. "That's my boy," he said. He raised his fist. "Now you're getting with it, son. Putting in the miles."

I shrugged. Didn't know what to say. "Well, I couldn't sleep," I said.

"That's good, son. Shows you're gearing up."

I went out the door. Somehow he'd taken the joy out of it.

People were still sleeping. Cars were parked along the streets. I jogged to the park. There was time to do a few miles before school. I thought of Cindy Watanabe and her marathon runs. She would have to be doing at least ten miles a day training for that ordeal.

I decided to do four miles, five times around. Any more would have made me late for school, and perhaps too tired for track practice later in the afternoon.

I did two easy laps at about half speed. Starting the third, I had company. The girl with the blond ponytail came running in from a small side street opposite the park. She cut in ahead of me without a smile or wave of recognition. Then I was losing ground, watching her go. The white top, red shorts, red shoes. The ponytail swinging from side to side.

She had about fifty yards on me when I cranked it up a little. When I drew closer, she picked up her pace, moving ahead with a steady, powerful stride.

Seeing her for the second time, I decided she was older than I'd first thought. Maybe in her twenties, a college girl. She ran like one. In the mile run, you try to come close to or beat four minutes. Middle distance runners run a little more slowly. But not much. The top marathon runners average under five-minute miles for the distance. The top woman marathoner, Grete Waitz of Norway, averages 5:33 per mile. Her time of 2:25:4 is the best in the world.

I didn't know how many laps this ponytail girl was going to do. I wondered if she was a runner in a girls' division I didn't know anything about.

Meanwhile I was pounding along, trying to do an easy workout run, falling farther and farther behind her.

I forgot my plan for a nice easy run. She had more than a hundred yards on me now. Something went off in my head, and I went after her.

The third time around I had gained half the distance between us. I still had two more laps for my four miles. I had never raced four miles, but it seemed I was going to learn how.

I opened up a little more, and by the end of the fourth time around, I was close. Her stride and pace hadn't eased off. She was rock steady in her rhythm. I gained because I began running harder.

As I started my fifth and last time around, the

girl still had about a twenty-five-yard lead. Okay, I told myself, there's almost a mile left. Make believe you're in a big race, and try to win it.

Halfway around, I had closed to about ten yards. If I went all out, I figured I had a chance to get by her just before the end. I remembered the trees. This time I wanted to be far enough ahead so there wouldn't be the same problem.

I was breathing hard, working hard. It wasn't going to be easy. And when I pulled up close to her heels, she surged ahead again. This girl was a real competitor. She wouldn't give me an inch. She wouldn't let anybody pass her.

She's also a little crazy, I thought. This isn't that serious or important, is it?

Our feet were thudding on the path, both of us letting it all out. Running as if it was the last race on earth for humans.

I got to her shoulder. Saw her steely eyes set straight ahead. Her mouth open, sucking air, her face drawn with the effort.

Now, I told myself, now. *Drive!*

I drew almost even with her, and then the trees loomed up ahead. It was ridiculous. The same dumb thing over again. If I stayed with her, one of us would have to run into the tree trunk.

I eased off. She sped ahead, the ponytail swinging

41

high. One more time around, I thought, and I might have got her. But my four miles were done. I still had to shower and have breakfast, go to school and have something left for Coach.

I jogged away, out of the park, getting my breath back. The girl in the red shoes was still running, her pace a bit slower than when she was fighting me off, but not that much slower. She was going to put in some more laps.

I jogged home, shaking my head. That girl must think I'm a regular quitter, I thought.

Pop had gone off to work by the time I got home. I took my shower and had some breakfast. I felt tired. Also very depressed. I wondered where all the fun was in running.

My bad luck held all day. I wasn't prepared to talk
about my book report when Mr. Robinson called
on me. I said I was still trying to get into it. He
gave me a funny look. Maybe he thought I was trying
to take advantage of him now that we'd had a
friendly conversation. When the bell rang ending
the English period, I grabbed my books and got out
of there fast.

Track was a total disaster. My legs were stiff and
felt as if somebody had poured lead into them during

the day. Coach Gordon had me all set for another good mile. Cott and Rose had fifty yards on me after three laps. I tried to go after them on the last lap. I ran as if I was standing still. Nothing hurt, but nothing was working either. Not daring to let myself quit, I ran it out. At the finish, they had over a hundred yards on me.

Cott and Rose came jogging back. Both stopped near where I was bent over trying to get my breath back.

"What happened, Wonder Boy?" Cott said. "Where was all that early speed?"

"I think he's saving it," Don Rose said grinning. "He's going to lay it on us at the meet next week."

"Is that a fact, Boy Wonder?" Jerry Cott said. "Is that your master plan—save now and spend later?"

I was shaking my head, feeling rotten. "No way. I'm still trying to convince everybody last time was an accident. I can't keep up with you guys."

Don Rose lost his friendly grin. "Listen, hotshot, don't give us that stuff. You ran four-ten, and that's good enough to beat anybody in the city. You did it once and you can do it again. Stop trying to play it for sympathy."

"But I'm not—" I started to say. Coach Gordon was whistling me over, waving his arms. I turned away, wondering what Coach was going to blast me with.

It didn't take long.

"Okay, Davis," he barked. "What happened to you out there? You ran as if somebody poured cement in your shoes."

"It felt like it, too, Coach. Honest," I said, "I just couldn't get going."

His eyes were steely bright. "You got a cold? Coming down with anything?"

I shook my head.

"You smoking? Drinking too many beers?"

I was shaking my head, wishing it would fall off and then he would lay off me. "No, Coach, none of the above. I mean, I don't smoke or drink beer. I don't know what it was. I just felt dead out there."

"Well, you ran like it, too," he said harshly. He put his finger out and leveled it off in front of my eyes. "Now I know your style, and I'm not going to let you backslide, understand? I won't have a quitter on my track team."

I started to say I wasn't a quitter, but something inside me told me to hold back. Don't be too sure about that, it said. I clammed up instead, not daring to say anything.

He gestured out to the track oval. "Okay, we don't

have to make a federal case about it. Maybe you're just not feeling right. That it?"

I nodded. It sounded reasonable. "Yeah, Coach, I guess."

"No problem," he said. "Now get out there and run a few more laps. That ought to get you out of it."

"How many, Coach?" I said.

He shrugged. "Take it easy on yourself. Make it three miles."

That's only twelve times around, I told myself, as I started off. You can do it. After all, you want to be a runner, right?

I had gone around five times before I remembered my early morning run in the park. I figured that was what took all the speed out of me. But I didn't think it would be a good idea to tell Coach. I didn't want to see him cry.

11

I was cutting across the school lot on my way home after the workout. Mr. Robinson was getting into his car. A tan Honda Civic. He saw me and waved. I dragged myself over.

"How was your workout?" he said.

"Terrible. I was dead. Couldn't move. If you dig slow motion, that was me out there."

He nodded. "It happens. Next time you'll do better."

I shrugged. "Maybe. You mean that used to happen to you, too?" I didn't know much about good trackmen. And I wasn't forgetting Mr. Robinson had been one of the very best, a champion runner, in his time.

"Of course. It happens to everybody. We all get stale every now and then. You'll see. Next time, you'll burn up the track."

"I don't know about that," I said. "All I ever did was that one good run in practice. There's a girl I meet running in the park. I haven't caught up to her yet."

He smiled. "Well, some girls are pretty good distance runners, too, you know. They're not that far behind the men. Do you know her name?"

"I haven't come close enough yet to find out," I said. "She doesn't kid around. She runs hard and fast."

"I wouldn't worry about it," he said. "Sounds as if she's had a lot of racing experience. Once you're into it, you see, you don't like to be beaten. By anybody. Even for fun."

"Is that what happened to you in college?" I said.

"Sure, I got beat. And I didn't like it. It wasn't like the old days when I was winning all my meets, breaking the school and city records, being the school hero. That's kind of nice, you know. Winning is always more fun than losing."

I shrugged. "I wouldn't know. So far I haven't done any of that winning." He seemed interested in talking about track, in no hurry to get home. "Maybe I never will. I guess you never had that problem."

He shook his head, his eyes smiling, yet far away. "No, I never had that problem. We're different personalities, you see. I'm not talking about speed, either. I have the feeling you think you can't beat anybody."

"Right on. Well, maybe my kid sister."

He laughed. "Well, there you are. That's the difference. You see, I thought I could beat anybody. Everybody. The world, in fact. And when I ran, that was it. To be the very best—ever."

"Wow, that's heavy," I said.

He shrugged. "Sure. But for a little while, I was. I made the dream come true. I really was the best." He threw out his hands, smiling wryly. "Not that it lasted very long."

"Well, a high school four-minute mile is still very good time, Mr. Robinson. And at least you got to your goal, what you wanted to do, or be."

He nodded. "True enough, Monty. But what about you? You seem to be giving up on yourself before you've even started. Before you've found out how good you are—or could be."

"Maybe it was different with you," I said. "You

49

were probably good from the start."

He held his hand up. "Hold it," he said. "I heard about your time the other day. A four-ten, right? Now that's real good time for any schoolboy."

"Where'd you hear that?"

He grimaced. "Coach Gordon and I have a few words now and then. What about it? Beat his two top men, he said."

"Not exactly. I had about ten yards on them, you know. I never did run the whole mile."

He was shaking his head. "It doesn't matter. You beat his two top seniors. One's a city record holder. It proves you're better than you think. The only one who doesn't believe that is you."

"Well, yeah. I got lucky that day. That's all I know."

"How do you expect to do in the dual meet?" he asked.

"I don't know," I said. "I don't expect to win, if that's what you mean. Cott and Rose are too good. They're both strong runners. Also I hear Culver has some pretty good guys."

He shrugged and got back into his little car. "I'm not trying to compare us. You don't have the need I had, to be the best. And perhaps I had more natural speed than you. But you'll never find out how good you are if you keep putting yourself down. That's what's important here."

I smiled. "Maybe it's safer that way."

He nodded. "Don't kid yourself. Everybody wants to win. I don't care if you win or not, but it's important that *you* care."

"The other day—"

He cut me off. "You know, it also takes courage to go all out, to try to do your very best—and risk losing."

He started his car, waved, and moved off. I stood rooted, unable to answer him. Hey, I told myself, did you get all that? It sounds like good advice. Maybe you're not a quitter. You're just not thinking right.

I went home thinking about it, a little more mixed up than usual.

12

It seemed to me that at first Mr. Robinson had given me good advice. To do what I wanted to do, to please myself, even if nobody else liked it. To dare to be unpopular. I kind of liked that idea.

Then he changed it on me. Do your best, he said. Find out how good you are. Otherwise you're only kidding yourself.

Well, maybe it had been fun for him, while it lasted.

But I didn't want to be the best in the world. I didn't want to beat everybody, or even feel that I had to. It didn't seem to matter to me whether I could or not. Why couldn't I just go on being me? Running because I liked to. Being an average runner—not the worst, not the best, but somewhere in between. Was that considered quitting?

That mystery runner in the park who had to beat me every time. What would happen if I beat her? Would she hang up her track shoes? Would she quit running?

I figured I could understand my pop. Because he'd been so good, he wanted me to be good, too. So that he could be proud of me, and know that he'd passed on his terrific running genes.

I could understand Coach Gordon, too. If I was a track coach, I guess I would want all my kids to win. That was what the job was all about, to turn out a good track team. Maybe if his team won more meets, he had a better chance of holding on to his job. Or maybe making more money on his next contract. That was okay. I'd read in the papers about coaches getting fired for having losing seasons. And getting big increases if their teams won. So that was okay. Coach Gordon had a contract to teach track at our school. And to prove he was worth the money, he had to show results. Our team had to put out, too, and try to win for him. That meant me, and everybody else.

Would he drop me from the team if I lost too many races? I didn't know. I wasn't getting paid. I'd volunteered. Just for the fun of it. And now somehow it wasn't such fun any more.

Would it be more fun if I got to be terrific and won all the time? I didn't think so. It would be an awful strain. If I won once, I would have to prove I could do it over and over again.

Well, anyway, I don't think we have to worry about that possibility, I told myself. Mr. Robinson's record is safe with you.

I was thinking about all this, going over and over it in my mind—going kind of crazy you might say—when the phone rang. It was Cindy Watanabe.

"I was just wondering," she began, "if your father would feel bad if you took me to the movies some night. You know, like, would I be taking you away from your training, and all?"

"It's not that," I said. "But it has to be the very best movie in L.A. Maybe in the whole state or in the whole world. It can't be just any old movie. It has to be the best. We don't want to waste our time on any movie that quits on us, do we?"

"You feeling okay?" she said.

"Not worse than rotten," I said. "Is that okay?"

"You're too young to be cracking up," she said. "What's your problem?"

"I don't know exactly," I said. "I think it's that I don't know who I am or what I'm supposed to be. Is that a problem?"

"Are you talking about running?"

"Well, sure," I said. "That dumb dual meet is coming up and I don't know if I'm going to disappoint a lot of people, or not."

"You're turning it into too big a deal," she said.

"I am?"

"Running is no problem," she said. "Actually, it's very simple."

"It is?"

"Right. All you have to do is lean forward and put one foot in front of the other."

"Is that all you think about when you run?"

"Well, not all, exactly," she said.

"Okay, what else?"

"I try not to think about my body falling off," she said.

13

Before she hung up, Cindy and I agreed that it would be a good idea for her to be taken to a movie Saturday night. It proved to me how intelligent Cindy Watanabe was because she got my mind away from thinking about myself. Then I began thinking about Cindy instead. I knew right away that was more fun. Also it's not easy to find a nice, intelligent girl who is also a very good runner.

That night I read the kid sister's book about mountain climbing. It gave me something new to think about. According to the man who wrote it, he didn't risk his neck climbing mountains just to get up to the top. He said he liked what he saw along the way.

He said it was like going through life zones. You start out in low altitudes which have a desertlike atmosphere. Higher up, there are crops that grow in more temperate climates. Then you reach an area where only wheat and barley and potatoes are grown, then a grazing area. Finally, there is a place where nothing grows at all, and there is your mountain.

I knew immediately I could relate that experience to running. The race was going to be my mountain. All I had to do was go through the wheat and barley and potatoes, first.

He also wrote that even the danger of climbing a 26,000-foot-high mountain in the Himalayas didn't bother him. He said that for the people who had experience and knew the mountain—the snow, ice, weather, and environment—it wasn't dangerous at all.

He mentioned an avalanche. It was coming right toward him, but at the last moment, it turned off in another direction. That proved to him, he said, that it didn't make sense to worry.

Okay, I told myself, you got that? Nothing like

ice or snow or rocks ever comes down on a runner in a track meet. Compared to scaling a mountain, running is kid stuff.

Before I fell asleep that night, I saw myself running. Cott and Rose were in there with me, and some other guys I didn't know. I was running nice and loose, not feeling any pain at all. I was feeling so good about it, I fell asleep before I found out who won.

In the dream that followed, I was climbing the highest peak in the world. Just when I was nearly at the top, I heard a terrible sound of tearing and rumbling. I looked up and there was this thing that looked like the whole mountain coming down on me.

It's okay, I told myself, it's only an avalanche. Nothing to worry about.

Are you kidding? I heard myself screaming. An avalanche is a lot to worry about. What are we going to do?

The other part of me was very cool, very logical. There's nothing to worry about because there isn't anything we can do about it, my inner voice said.

I couldn't believe this nut of an other self I had. I looked around. I was on a narrow ledge. There really wasn't any place to go. Except out into space.

The avalanche was coming closer, almost in slow

motion. I could feel my heart tighten, freezing up with fear. The roaring sound got louder and louder.

I was covering my face with my hands when at the last possible moment the roaring stopped. I was so shaken, I woke up. I was sweating and shaking, looking all around my bed for the snow and ice and big rocks.

Then suddenly the roaring sound began again. I looked out the window. It was our next-door neighbor going around his grass lawn with a power mower.

There goes your avalanche, I told myself. That guy was right, after all.

14

It was Saturday morning. I got out of bed and into my track shoes and shorts. As I began to jog down the street to the park, I wondered why our neighbor was up so early mowing his lawn. Maybe he's got some kind of a big race coming up, I told myself, and he can't sleep either.

I had the park all to myself until Cindy Watanabe showed up. She was running toward me, her skin glistening as if she'd been running for some time. She was wearing a red headband to catch the sweat from coming down into her eyes.

"So this is where you run," she said. "I had to do five miles to get here."

"I'm just starting," I said. "We can do a few miles around this park, if you like."

She looked around at the level park area and shook her head. "Too easy," she said. "I need a good workout." She pointed ahead. "Hey, those look like pretty good hills."

I knew about those good hills, which was one reason I ran around the park instead. "That first one is a half mile up," I told her.

"Terrific," she said. "Let's go."

I knew if I hesitated for a single second, Cindy would ask me if I wanted to run home and ask my pop for permission first to run the hills. "Okay," I said, and ran alongside her, in stride with her easy gait.

We were crossing the street when the blond ponytail girl came around the corner. She and Cindy raised their arms and waved, smiling their greetings. Then the ponytail cut into the park and was behind us.

"Do you know her?" I said.

"Do I?" said Cindy. "I love her so much, I hate her. That's Julie Mars. She's the top girl marathoner on the west coast. She only runs it about two hours faster than I do."

61

"No kidding," I said, suddenly feeling a lot better. "Is she that good?" We were starting up the hill, and I wondered if I had to stop talking now and save my energy for the steep grade.

Cindy was leaning forward, getting herself balanced on the incline. Her legs were driving and I knew I was in big trouble. She was going to really run up this monster hill.

"She does around two-forty," Cindy said. "That's only about thirty minutes off the best men's time. So you know Julie's good."

"I knew it before you told me," I said. "Every time I meet her in the park, she goes past me like I'm standing still."

Cindy was smiling and chugging along. I was happy to see the hill was slowing her down some. "Well, what do you expect?" she said. "She's a champion."

I knew it, I told myself. No wonder she beat you.

We got to the top of the hill and went flying down. I hoped Cindy had had it now with hills, but she was pointing to another one.

"Hey, that one looks even better," she said.

In my opinion, it looked a lot worse. But then I'm not one of those crazy girl marathon runners who really like to suffer.

That night was the night I was taking Cindy Watanabe to the flicks. I asked my pop if I could borrow
his car.

He looked at me. "Do you have a driver's license?"
I shook my head. "No."
"Do you know how to drive?"
"Well, not exactly."
He opened his newspaper. "Case closed," he said.
I took the bus.

16

It was a science-fiction movie, *Brogg's Brain*, about a world of the future. Brogg, a great scientist, couldn't keep himself from dying of old age after he got to be two hundred. He knew of a way to keep his brain alive. He had his friends put it into some kind of electronic box after his death, hidden deep inside a cave. Then a man who'd always wanted to be ruler came into power. But he was a dictator and a mean dude. He passed laws to control the people, but old Brogg's brain kept sending out different orders, which everybody was obeying. The new dictator couldn't find out where the brain was hidden and was going nuts.

I leaned over to whisper to Cindy. "I don't get it," I said. "Why do they all do what that old brain in the box says?"

"I don't know," she whispered back. "I think mostly because this is a very dumb movie. Those people up there believe Brogg had a terrific brain. He has them all hypnotized."

"You're right," I said. "It's a real dumb movie. Why did we come here?"

"Because you wanted to see it," Cindy said.

"That's right," I said. "I did, didn't I?"

"But it's not your fault. I wanted to see it, too. I hate dumb movies."

"Me, too," I said. "Next time I pick a movie for us, remind me what happened this time."

"I'll probably forget. And next time you decide to take me out, you'll probably get it wrong in your memory cells, and think it was all my fault we went to this dumb movie."

"No, I won't," I said. "I'll probably give up movies, instead. This hurts more than running."

"I could have done five miles by now," Cindy said.

Somebody spoke loudly behind us. "Say, would you kids mind not talking? We're trying to listen to this movie."

"If we left now," Cindy said, "we could have a nice juicy hamburger."

"I think I feel more like a taco or burrito," I said.

"Hey," this voice behind us said. "Would you kids mind?"

Cindy got up. She turned to the voice behind us. "I'm sorry we disturbed you," she said. "Do you really like this dumb movie?"

The man yelled back. "I don't care if I like it or not. I came here to see it, and all I hear is you kids talking."

I made my voice very polite. "I'm really sorry we disturbed your seeing the movie. We're leaving now."

"Well, hurry up," he said. "Your head's in the way."

17

"Speaking of that dumb Brogg's brain," Cindy said, "you can improve your running by hypnotizing yourself."

"How do I do that?" I said.

We were finishing up our burger, burrito, and soft drink at the fast-food place near the movie. The only brilliant thing I had done in picking that particular movie was to guarantee we would share the same bus home.

Cindy wiped her lips. There was a little spot of

ketchup on her nose. I couldn't make up my mind how to break the news to her. There's some ketchup on your nose, I could say. In which case, she would wipe it off with her napkin. Or I could say, "Lean forward," and when she did I would wipe it off myself. I didn't know any more about girls than I did about winning track and field events. I let the ketchup stay. Maybe it would fall off by itself, or evaporate. I decided if it didn't do anything before we left, I would take a stand about it, one way or another.

Cindy's mind wasn't being ruined by ketchup so she remembered what she wanted to tell me about hypnotism. "You create mental images," she said. "You see yourself in a winning situation. Your form is better, your stride is better, you breathe better, and best of all, you can actually see yourself going past people, winning."

"You want me to practice lying to myself," I said.

"You're the most negative person sometimes," she said. "It might be your time to win next week. Everybody else might have torn hamstrings or bad heels or tendons. If you happen to be the only healthy one in the race, just think how easy it would be to win."

"That makes more sense," I said. "Unless when I'm doing my self-hypnotism, I pull a muscle myself passing all those other dudes."

"Be like Brogg," she said. "Dominate the scene with your brain."

"I'll work on it," I said. The clock on the wall said it was time to get going to make the 10:32 bus. Cindy saw it, too, and got up. "There's some ketchup on your nose," I said.

She crossed her eyes, looking down. "Where?"

I got my napkin and brushed it off without bloodying her nose. "There. It's okay now."

"Thanks," she said.

"That's okay. I just happened to notice it." I wondered why, without ever having to practice, I was a better liar than a runner.

She took my arm while we walked to the cashier. That made it harder to get at the money in my pocket. I wondered how many buses I could afford to let go by before telling Cindy I needed that arm.

"I've noticed," Cindy said, "that you don't have a nice, steady girl friend."

I looked down at her arm on mine. "What ever gave you that idea?" I said.

The bus came along. We rode to the last stop. The driver had to tell us to get off. He wanted to get home.

18

Pop was talking to me. "That girl who calls you— her name is Watanabe?"

"That's right. Cindy Watanabe."

"Sounds Japanese," he said.

"Yeah, pop. Cindy is Japanese, all right. Third generation in L.A."

He looked at me over his newspaper. "You like her?"

"You bet. Cindy's a real neat girl."

He put his face down into the paper again. "There

must be some neat American girls around, too—right?"

"Sure, pop. Lots. Why do you ask? Cindy is as American as I am. She happens to be of Japanese descent."

"Just curious," he mumbled. "No particular reason."

Yeah, sure, I thought. Butt out of my life, I wanted to say, only I couldn't.

"Cindy runs the marathon, pop," I said. "She's run five already. That's five more than I can do. Maybe you, too, huh?"

He put his paper down, head cocked. His face looking interested now. "No kidding," he said. "Five, you said? Say, that's pretty good for a girl."

"Darn good, pop. Twenty-six miles. I bet I couldn't go half the distance."

He was shaking his head, his lips pursed. "Sure you could, son. Just a matter of practice, you know. You can get your body used to anything."

"Yeah, I guess. She runs ten miles a day. Over seventy miles a week."

He stared. More head shaking. "Say, that is a lot. She your age?"

"Just about. Maybe a few months younger."

He cleared his throat. "That's very good. But in my day, you know, we didn't have the know-how.

They've got all the numbers in now. Know what the body can take." He showed me his smile. "Practice makes perfect, you know."

"I guess," I said. "I may get into it, one of these days. Sounds like one tough challenge."

He waved his hand at me. "Well, now, hold on. You have more important things to take care of. You've got to be thinking of your mile run, Monty. Thursday, isn't it?"

I nodded. "You know it," I said.

"I'll be there," he said. "Rooting you in."

It was my turn to stare. "You're taking off work?"

"Why not?" he said. "How often do I get a chance to see my son run away with the field?"

"But gee, pop, it's only a crummy dual meet. We've got our two top milers in it, Cott and Rose. Culver has some good guys, too, I hear. Doing around four-fourteen. I don't see myself running away from that field. I'll be lucky if I can stay on the same track with them."

He looked at me sternly. "Now that's the kind of talk I never like to hear, son. Nobody ever won anything with that kind of negative attitude."

I was getting hot. My voice rose. "Well, I'll be in it, sure. Trying my best. But don't you be expecting me to win. Because you're liable to be disappointed."

He tried to soothe me. "Now son—"

"Now nothing," I said. Nearly screaming now. "Those guys are good, I keep telling you. Rose has been close to four-ten and Cott's been there. Four-ten. You hear that?"

"So what?" he said. "You've done it yourself."

I stared. Shaken. "Where did you hear that?"

He shrugged, smiling. "Well, don't get mad. But I check with your coach every once in a while. He fills me in, son. He knows I'm interested. Coach Gordon tells me—"

I never let him finish. "You've got no right to be checking with him. That time I did was a fluke. An accident. I never even ran the full mile—"

He was shaking his head, smiling harder. "I know, son. Coach Gordon explained that part of it, too. Also the way you feel about it. But he and I both know one thing you haven't taken into account."

I didn't want to know what that was. But I asked, anyway. "Like what?"

"That extra ten yards you didn't do—all it amounts to is another second or two. So you can figure you did a four-eleven, four-twelve. Don't you realize city meets have been won with those numbers?"

I looked at him. He looked at me. There were a lot of things I wanted to say, only I didn't know how to say them.

"I'm going out for a walk," I said.

73

I was at the door. His voice was louder, reaching me across the room. "I've been through it all," he said, his voice rumbling. "You've got the right stuff in you. When that starter's gun goes off, you'll be right out in front with the leaders. And coming down to the finish, you'll be out in front and they'll be eating your dust. I know it!"

I was shaking when I got outside. That mountain climber who went through the wheat and barley and potatoes to get to the mountain never met anybody like my old man.

I was too mad to walk straight. I had so much steam inside, I was bubbling over. I began running.

I went around the park once, but that wasn't enough. I crossed the street and found the hill I had run up with Cindy. I charged up that. It helped a little, that hill. The trouble was, I was so mad, I was crying.

Footsteps sounded behind me. I turned my head. It was the ponytail girl, the marathon runner, Julie Mars. What does she want now, I thought angrily. It's *my* hill.

She raised her arm, smiling. "Wait up," she called. "I'll run with you."

Me wait up for her? That was a new one. I slowed. I didn't realize I'd been running that hard.

She came up beside me. "I didn't know you worked hills," she said.

"I don't, really," I said. "I'm just trying them out."

She was watching my stride. "Lean forward more," she said. "Be part of the grade."

I did that. Not mad anymore.

She nodded. "A little more spring, some bounce. You're slogging it. Bring your knees up higher."

I did that, too. It helped.

"Way to go," she said. "Let's do it."

We went side by side up the steep hill. I was breathing hard and hoped she wouldn't notice. We ran evenly to the top. She waved left for the downgrade.

"Now you've got to put your weight back more on your heels," she said.

I tried that. It felt better. We were flying down the hill. The wind whipped my face. I was beginning to feel good.

"Are you training for the marathon?" she asked.

I shook my head. "I'm a miler. I'm trying to get ready for a dual meet Thursday."

"A miler?" she said. "Terrific. You'll help me build up my speed."

I looked at her. She was serious. "Well," I said.

"You were the boy running with Cindy the other day," she said.

"Yeah. She told me about you." I grinned. "No wonder I couldn't beat you to that tree."

We turned off at the bottom of the hill. Then we were running along a level street. She pointed far off to a street light. "That light there. No trees in the way. How about it—or are your legs gone?"

I shook my head. "You mean run all out?"

She laughed, her head thrown back. "It's the only way to fly," she said.

"Say when," I said.

She counted off her fingers, and said "Go!" I let her take a three-step lead, and then I went at it.

It was about a half-mile run. I was so wound up, I guess I went crazy. We ran shoulder to shoulder for only a few steps, and then I went by. I kept digging, expecting her to come on. My feet were flying.

She made a good effort, her feet thudding behind me. But I never let up, and when I got to the light, there was a lot of distance between us.

She came up panting, not breaking her stride until she reached the mark. Then she bent over, gasping for breath. When she caught it, she stood up straight. Her hand clapped me on the shoulder.

"Oh, thank you, thank you," she said. "That was terrific."

I grinned, not knowing what to say. "Well, I guess it's more my distance."

She shook her head. "Don't give me that, young man. You're a very good runner."

"Let's hope it lasts till Thursday," I said.

"It will," she said. "Now no more hill work until then. Just keep working on your speed. A lot of fast intervals. Two-hundreds, three-hundreds. And some real short ones for your finishing kick. Sixty yards or so."

"How many?" I said.

She grinned. "Are you kidding? All you can do and still walk home. Up till the day before—that's your easy day."

"Thanks, Julie," I said.

"Thank *you*," she said. "After your meet, maybe we can do it again." She was looking off, ready to go again.

"Swell," I said.

"And if it's in the park," she said, "the tree is yours."

She waved and ran off.

I felt better by the time I got home. Hearing it

from the ponytail girl made all the difference. Did she say you were a very good runner? I asked myself.

I nodded, smiling, and thumped my chest. "You better believe it!"

I don't know what came over me the next few days. I studied like crazy. I worked out hard. I killed myself over and over again. It's Brogg's brain, I told myself. He's reaching you. Making sure you do it right.

I'd finish a tough run. Blow out and say, "How was that, Brogg? How did I do?" I could hear him in my mind saying, "More. Do more. More, more, more."

"Slave driver," I said.

Well, you do tend to blow your mind if you're a jock. I could see glimpses of it in my old man. All that hard running blows your brain apart, I guess.

I wrote up my book report and handed it in. Mr. Robinson looked surprised. "What's this?" he said. "I thought you were saving it all for your mile run."

"I'm just going through the wheat, barley, and potatoes," I said. "I haven't got to the mountain yet."

He stared at me. "Whatever that means, it sounds pretty good."

I pointed to the book report. "It's all in there. Only I'm not going to burn out like you did. I'm only going to the mountain one time. And I'll do it right."

He stared, shaking his head. "Okay. We'll talk about it, if you like."

I laughed. Feeling spaced out. Jabbing my finger in the air again at the book report on his desk. "That book on mountain climbing, and a rotten movie called *Brogg's Brain*. That did it. Also Julie Mars."

His head cocked. "I know that name."

"The marathon girl. She's some runner."

"Of course," he said. "Do you know her?"

"Well, not really," I said. "She's somewhere between the wheat and barley. Or maybe between the barley and the potatoes."

Mr. Robinson put his hand up. "I think I'm getting a headache. Nice talking to you, Monty."

"Well, that's only *your* opinion," I said.

21

"How we doing?" Cindy said.

"Hey, are you the girl who calls with a Japanese name?"

"I guess so. Why?"

"My pop thinks you're Japanese."

"No kidding?" she said. "I wish somebody had told *me.*"

"He thinks I should find a nice American girl."

"And what do you think?"

"I think I'd like to see *Brogg's Brain* again with you."

"That dumb movie? Why would you want to see that dumb movie ever again?"

"Because it made everything else seem so perfect."

"You've got a point. When do you want to do all this?"

"Next week. After the meet. Okay?"

"I don't know. Do you expect we'll get along better this time?"

"You mean there's better?"

"Okay," she said. "You talked me into it."

22

Coach Gordon didn't know that a man could leave his brain in a box and give orders without raising his voice. "Move it, Davis," he yelled. "Lift those feet. You're supposed to be running, not roller skating."

When I finished the run, he was looking at the watch in his hand. Shaking his head. Nice big frown. "Four-twenty again! You know I'm almost ready to believe you when you say your four-ten was an accident."

"Well, sure," I said, catching my breath. "I tried

to tell you. Your watch was seeing things."

"Maybe," he said, glaring. "But I know you can do better. Your stride is good and your wind is good. So what else is there?"

I waited, figuring he would tell me.

He came through. Tapping his chest. "Heart. That's what's missing. Heart. You've got to want to win."

"Yes, sir," I said.

"Your old man can give you pointers on that," he said. "He was a scrapper."

"Yeah, I guess," I said. "Did you know him when he was a sprinter back in the old days?"

"What old days?" he barked. "He's not an old man yet. Neither am I. We went to high school together."

"No kidding?" I said. "Was he really fast?"

He looked angrily at me. "Well, why do you think I'm on your back so much? Of course, he was fast. He worked his butt off, too, getting that way. That's why I figure you can do it, too. You're his kid, aren't you?"

"Yes, sir," I said. "There's always the chance, though, that he didn't pass on those fast genes."

"I'm not worried about that," he growled. "I'm coming back to the gumption factor. You've got to want to win. If you don't have that, in my book you're a jellyfish."

I wondered why a jellyfish's old man never bothered to straighten the kid fish out about that. "Yes, sir," I said. "Well, I'll work on it, Coach. No kidding. I'll try my best. In fact, if I don't do real good soon, I'll take myself off the track team, and you can concentrate on the other guys who are good."

He levelled his finger at me. "Now don't be quitting on me again. If I want you off the track team, I'm the one to make the decision, not you. I don't want Scrappy Davis thinking I didn't give his kid a chance."

"Was that his name—Scrappy Davis?"

Coach looked at me disgustedly. "I thought you knew that. Now get out of here and do some more laps before I lose my mind."

"Yes, sir," I said. "How many?"

He surprised me this time. "Suit yourself, Davis. You've got till Thursday to work it all out with yourself."

I went out and did some more laps. I didn't bother to count them this time. I just did them until I couldn't do any more.

On the way home, I was talking to myself again. Well, you may not be such a terrific runner. But at least your nickname isn't Scrappy Davis.

23

The kid sister came into my room. I was doing my homework at the desk. She flopped on my bed. "Boy, are you in trouble," she said.

"I guess that's the good news," I said. "What's the bad?"

"It's all bad," she said. "My friend—the one I told you about whose brother goes to Culver—told me he's under four-ten in the mile. Are you anywhere near that?"

I shrugged. "Maybe I'll be near enough to wave

87

when he goes by. What's his name?"

"Ellison," she said. "Bunny Ellison."

"Figures," I said. I reached for another textbook.

"Well, aren't you worried?"

"Why should I worry? He's the one named Bunny, not me. Let him worry."

"I don't get it," she said. "Lots of kids have weird nicknames."

"Yeah, I guess so," I said. "Do you mind not having one?"

"I don't know," she said. "There's nothing special enough about me to rate a nickname. What do you think?"

I thought about it. "Well, you have a pretty good temper. Maybe you could use a nickname like Scrappy."

She looked delighted. "Scrappy? Hey, that's neat. Yeah, Monty, I like that. Thanks a lot."

"It's okay," I said.

"I can't wait to tell pop," she said, going out.

"He'll get a big kick out of that," I said.

In life, I've noticed, you don't get too many chances for these sensational ideas.

24

Cindy and I were having a soda at The Thirst House.

"Will you still like me even if I get beat in that race tomorrow?" I said.

"I don't know," she said.

"Well, I guess I'll get over it. It's not as if we've ever been married, or anything."

"That reminds me," she said. "If we ever do decide to get married, would you allow me to keep my maiden name?"

"Which one is that?"

"The Japanese name. Watanabe."

"I don't know, Cindy. It sounds awfully Japanese, don't you think?"

"Maybe. But it's the only one my father gave me."

"What was your mother's maiden name?"

"Igasaki."

"I think my father would like that one better. But not too much."

"Well, you can kid about it," Cindy said. "But it really bugs me that your father objects to my Japanese name. Where's he been?"

"Who?" I said. "You mean, old Scrappy Davis?"

She looked at me. Her mysterious smile got wider. Our eyes met and locked.

"No kidding?"

"No kidding. Scrappy Davis."

"Where did you hear that—for a fact, I mean?"

"Coach Gordon let it slip. He knew Pop in the old days. They went to school together."

"You know," she said smiling, "I really should marry you out of spite."

"You mean, so that we can use your name along with mine?"

"Better still, mine alone. They're doing that, you know."

"Hey, that's terrific. You mean, we could answer the phone that way, and all?"

"You bet."

"Terrific, Cindy," I said. "Will you marry me?"

"Well, you're only fifteen," she said. "Ask me again in about ten years."

It was a weird conversation. But Cindy and I accomplished a lot without having to go through words.

25

The night before the dual meet, I was stretched out on my bed thinking. Pop walked in. He sat down on my desk chair. "Just wanted to check with you, son. How are you feeling? Ready to whop 'em?"

"Well, I'm not up to that part yet, pa. Just thinking."

He edged the chair a little closer. Leaning forward. "That's good, son. Keep your mind on it. That's all a race is. It's concentration. Your best effort all put together."

"Sounds like a good idea," I said.

"You bet it is, Monty. And in case it's been running through your mind that this is just a dinky little dual meet, and not worth putting out a real effort, I'll tell you something. Sure, it's not like the big city or state meet, with all the top competition. But it's there, you see. Another challenge."

I looked at him. His face was red and sweating. He was so serious, I didn't feel like kidding with him. I thought I might as well go along with him, so that he would get it off his chest, and leave me alone to my brooding.

I remembered Mr. Robinson telling me how he had felt. That he had to be the best in the world. That he could beat anybody. Everybody. It seemed kind of weird to me that someone would think that way. Then I realized suddenly that my pop probably thought along the same lines. It was dumb of me not to have seen it before.

So I said, "I guess you liked those challenges when you were running, huh, pop?"

He nodded, grim-faced. "You bet your sweet life I did. And I'll let you in on a little secret I had that helped." He waved his hands as I didn't jump right in and beg him for it. "I know," he said. "You want to do things your own way. I come on sounding like someone from the year one. But running hasn't changed. The fastest guy still wins, doesn't he?"

I nodded. "So I'm told," I said.

"All right. Now get this," he said. "I won a lot on my speed, sure. But I also won a lot because of another thing."

He waited me out. Finally I said, "Okay, I'm listening."

"Okay. You know how it is at these meets. They all line up around the starting line. Everybody shaking hands, laughing. Trying to get loose. You know? Exchanging names. Wishing the other guy luck. You know?"

I nodded to let him know I knew.

"Okay," he said. "That's what they all did. But not me, not yours truly. I didn't take anybody's hand. I didn't wish anybody luck. I wasn't dancing around, shaking myself out with them, playing Mr. Nice Guy." His eyes were on me, but seemed far away.

"You didn't," I said.

He pounded a big fist into his open hand. "No, sir. I let those guys know from the start, this was competition. This was a race. The best guy would win. I didn't want them to be my buddies. I hated them all. They were my enemies. Anybody who could stop me from winning was my enemy. You see?"

I nodded. I got it.

"And that made them all a little uptight. Which suited me fine. I wanted them to know it would take the best anybody had to beat me."

"Did you really feel you could beat anybody?" I said.

He surprised me by shaking his head. "No, I was never that cocky. As a matter of fact, I wasn't that good. What I'm saying is that I won most of my races because I made myself hate everybody so much, I had to beat them. And I put that kind of pressure on them, and believe it or not, it made a lot of them fold.

"They couldn't take this hate I turned on them. I think it was fear, actually. That little bit of fear, because I was so deadly serious about it. That's what I'm trying to pass on to you. I don't know if you can do it, but it's worth a try. If you look like a winner, they let you go by."

"Well, maybe it worked for you. But I don't think I'd fool anybody. I don't have that attitude you had, pop. Sorry about that."

He got off the chair, nodding and rubbing his hands. "That's okay. I don't expect you to change overnight. But a lot of funny things happen in a race. The best guys don't always win, you know.

"Sometimes they get lost in the strategy, especially in the mile run. They don't know whether to set the pace or lay back and let the other guy do it. Or they have their mind set on watching one guy, and somebody else comes up with a better kick. More stamina. I've seen it happen."

"Okay, pop. Thanks," I said. "I'll try not to let you down."

He stood at the doorway, glowering. "Now hold on. You have it wrong. It's not me you'll be letting down. It's your own sweet self. I ran my races."

"Okay," I said. "We'll see what happens."

"Now you're talking," he said. Waving his fist. "And remember—every guy out there is your enemy."

I put the light out later and wondered about that.

Cindy told me not to worry. I could always grow a beard and nobody would know it was me who had dishonored the school.

"I can't grow a beard. I mean, I've tried but nothing happens."

"Well, I can always get you one of my ancestor's swords. They call it *hara-kiri*. All you do is fall on your sword."

"Forget it. I'll try growing the beard again."

"Listen," she said, "is it really that important?"

"I didn't think so before. But now it is, somehow. I can't even kid about it now. I'm so nervous I'm in shock."

"Listen, idiot," she said. "What's the worst that can happen?"

"I lose by a lot."

"And what's the best that can happen?"

"I lose by only a little."

"Next time I'll ask better questions. Meanwhile, I'll be the girl in the stands having a heart attack."

"Oh, come on, Cindy. It's not that important. It's only a dumb race."

"Well, why can't you remember that?"

"Okay. I'll remember that."

"And if you lose, get lost. I never want to speak to you again, dummy."

"Okay, okay," I said. "I get the message."

"I'm thinking way past this point. When you call me ten years from now, I won't even remember your name."

"Hey, is that possible? After I bought you a hamburger and a soft drink?"

"You're darn right it's possible. You want to know what else is possible?"

"No. What?"

"You might even win this dumb race."

"Well, yeah, sure. That's possible, all right."

"And on that note, I'll say good night. Don't forget where we were. It's possible. Anything is possible."

"I wonder if I'll be able to sleep tonight," I said.

"I don't think that's possible," Cindy said.

27

It was a cool Thursday afternoon. It looked like rain in the morning. But it always looks like rain in the morning in L.A.

I wonder why it always looks like rain in the morning in L.A., I said to myself.

That's how I started my big day.

Even though it wasn't possible, I'd fallen asleep. You see, I told myself, you can do anything.

Mom asked me what I wanted for breakfast. "What

I usually have," I told her. She reminded me I usually didn't have anything.

"It's a new day and a new beginning," I told her. I sat down at the table.

Mom looked at me nervously. "I feel as if we've just been married. You're like a total stranger. I don't even know what you like to eat."

"What does pop eat?"

"Bacon and eggs. Ham and eggs. Toast. Coffee."

I slapped the tablecloth. "Okay. I'll have the same."

"How about some oatmeal and milk instead?"

"You've got yourself a deal," I said.

She got busy with the boxes and pots. "Your father said to tell you he might not be able to make it. Some business appointment he may not be able to get out of."

"Oh, darn," I said. "And I was looking forward to it."

28

Culver is a ratty school in a ratty neighborhood. The kids there hate everybody so much they turn out terrific teams for all sports. They always win all-city in football and basketball. And because they're always running away from gang members or cops, they do well in track, too.

Coach Gordon looked around, sniffing. "I think this is the place where the starter keeps real bullets in his gun."

Our pole vaulter Cummings came over, dragging his long pole. "Hey, Coach," he said. "I hear they steal things here. Where can I put this thing?"

"No problem, Cummings," Coach said. "Take the pole with you."

"But, Coach. I gotta go to the john."

"That should be interesting," Coach said. "The rest of you kids follow me."

He took us into the Culver school gym. There were long wooden benches running in front of the lockers. We put down our gym bags.

Coach called across the room to a Culver kid. "Hey, how do we lock these things?"

The kid shrugged. "It don't make any difference. We break into them anyhow."

Coach whistled to Jarvis, our big shot-putter. "Jarvis, you got that big steel ball with you?"

Jarvis lifted his bag. "Right here, Coach."

"Good," Coach said. "After the guys put their stuff in the lockers, I want you to stay on guard here. If anybody tries to break in, you let them have it with your ball."

Jarvis looked horrified. "But, Coach. I might kill somebody."

"Well, yeah, that's a possibility," Coach said. "But your aim isn't too good with that thing. You'll miss a lot of them."

"What about my event? How do I get to do that?" Jarvis said.

"We'll call you. And we'll round up some volunteers from the student body to take your place. I'll send out for some hand grenades and a couple of machine guns, and maybe we can hold them off."

Even in my warm-up suit, my knees felt cold. You've got a misplaced case of cold feet, I told myself.

Cott and Rose were warming up. I knew what they looked like. I kept trying to find Bunny Ellison, their whiz-kid miler. When somebody pointed him out, I was sorry I'd asked. He was about six two and weighed about two hundred. That's not bad for a fifteen-year-old schoolboy.

Plus he looked mean and ugly. I wondered how I was going to scare *him.* Also, after you go to school in Culver, nothing can scare you anymore.

The kids from Culver filled the stands. "Maybe the gangs work later—special hours," Coach said.

We had a thin group of rooters from our school. They huddled together. They knew all about the mean, tough dudes from Culver High. I wondered if they'd be brave enough to cheer.

There were some speeches, some whistles, some catcalls and handclaps, and the meet got under way.

The 100-yard dash took longer than usual. When the starter raised his gun and fired it, two of the Culver guys hit the ground and rolled over. They thought somebody was shooting at them. The starter had to fire two more blanks to bring the other sprinters back. The next time he fired, someone in the Culver bleachers fired a gun, too. I smelled pot.

"Creeps," Coach Gordon muttered, scowling. "They always were a bunch of creeps."

It turned out that Coach had hated Culver for over sixty dual meets and about twenty-five years. He had competed against their guys in high school.

After two false starts, the Culver principal had to make an address on the speaker system. He told the crowd that if they didn't stop shooting, the dual meet would have to be forfeited to Emerson. He added that anybody smoking pot was in violation of the school honor system. That got a big laugh.

But Culver won the 100. And they won the 220. Then they ran away with the 440.

"Don't worry, guys," Coach Gordon said, "they're just lucky."

The Culver coach, Jesse Pauley, was laughing. Yelling over to Coach, asking him how he was doing. That was a dumb question because anybody could see how we were doing. Terrible.

"Remind me after the meet to punch Pauley in the nose," Coach said. "He's no sportsman."

In the 880, one of our guys bumped a Culver guy, and we won the event. A fight broke out in the stands.

In the mile relay, Culver was winning. But their lap runner dropped his stick, and we won. The kid claimed one of our guys knocked it out of his hands. The referee said no foul, because he didn't see it. Another fight broke out in the stands.

Then they ran some girls' events. They ran the 100, 440, and 880. I decided I'd better go to the john. While I was in there, I heard the announcement over the loudspeaker for the girls' two-mile run. When I came out, I heard the announcement of the winner.

Cindy Watanabe. Emerson High School. Time 10.44.8.

I didn't know she was running. I wondered if I

107

was too young to commit suicide. Maybe I could talk Big Jake Jarvis into throwing his shot at me.

I rushed over to congratulate Cindy. "I didn't know you were entered," I screamed. "You never told me you were running."

"Well, I didn't think I was," Cindy said, "but our coach talked me into it. She said our team could use the points."

"No kidding?" I said. "Is that the truth?"

"Well, not exactly," Cindy said.

A security guard came up and said I'd better clear out unless I wanted to run the girls' 110 low hurdles.

The announcer began talking about the field events coming up. Long jump. High jump. Triple jump. Shot put.

"Some of you guys go back and get Jarvis," Coach said. "He's got to start warming up."

They found Jarvis tied up. Stuffed in a locker.

Some Culver dudes had stolen his twelve-pound shot.

30

The mile run was coming up. My breakfast had already done that. I felt drained and tired and the race hadn't even started. It's just nerves, I told myself. Relax, it's only a little race. Less than five minutes out of your life.

Everybody was warming up, each with his own routine. Stretching. Jogging. Bending and twisting, trying to get loose. I kept moving, running up and down the track. It seemed as if I'd already run about eighteen miles. If you don't win, I told myself, at least you'll be in shape for a marathon.

I looked at Bunny Ellison doing little warmup bursts. His stride was awesome, about ten feet. I didn't want to go to the john again. I might not come out.

Cott and Rose were jogging up and down. I watched Cott enviously. He's so smooth you can develop an ulcer looking at him. Everything is perfect. His stride is long and even. His shoulders don't move. He doesn't seem to breathe. It all looks effortless. He floats along as if he's being pulled by an invisible string.

All the Culver runners looked big and strong. Why did you go out for track? I asked myself. You probably could have been a champion bird watcher. Nobody runs over bird watchers.

The tape replay set inside my head switched on. My old man was giving me his pep talk about hating. "They're all your enemy," he said.

Thanks, pop, I said silently. Only I want to do this my way.

Hating might be too easy, I told myself. You might get real good at it, and then where would you be? You want to go through your life hating?

Mr. Robinson was inside my head, telling me to risk losing. "Try your very best," he was saying again. "What have you got to lose?" He waited for an an-

swer and then added, "Don't kid yourself. Everybody wants to win. Everybody wants to win. Everybody wants to win—"

I switched him off. "It's okay, Mr. Robinson," I
whispered. "I get the message."

How would Albert Schweitzer handle this? I asked
myself. He knew all about suffering.

I waited for Dr. Schweitzer to get inside my head
and give me some sound tips. Nothing happened.
He had bigger problems to worry about.

Anyway, he's dead, I reminded myself. Stay with
the living. What would *you* like to do about this?

Well, I'd like to give it a shot, I said.

The other part of me didn't argue. *You're talking
about winning, I guess.*

Why not? I thought. Somebody has to win. It might
as well be me.

You did four-ten, I reminded myself. That's not
bad. Even with the little lead you had, you beat Cott
and Rose.

So why can't we do it again? I asked.

I waited for an answer and there wasn't any.

I was running a little harder now, breaking into
a sweat. *Okay, okay. That's enough of the warmup
stuff. Now let's get ourselves straight about thinking.*

Thinking about what?

When the answer came, I was ready.

Winning.

I looked across the track at Ellison. I looked at Cott and Rose. Those guys didn't know it, but they were in trouble.

31

The stands were buzzing. Everybody always gets up for the mile run. It's one of the few events where luck isn't a factor. If you get off slow, you can make it up. If you're away too fast, you can come back to the field. And if you're good, the crowd knows it and gets behind you and roots you in.

The announcer called the event and gave our names over the sound system. The starter waved us to the line. I walked over, not the same person I had been only moments before. Coach Gordon had landed a little surprise on me. And I wasn't the cool cat I had prepared myself to be. Instead I was shaking with anger.

In track meets, they give the most points for winning. But you get points for placing second and third. If your team places second and third in an event, the points add up to the same as for first place.

Coach was scowling, going over some numbers on a paper. "They've got us fifty-two to forty-nine, Davis. You'll have to be a rabbit."

Don't get mad, I told myself. He doesn't know you just psyched yourself into being the best miler here. He thinks you're still the jerk who tells everybody how awful he is, and how he just runs because he likes to run, and so on.

I said, "How do you mean, Coach?"

He waved his hands. "Look, there's you, Cott, and Rose. Culver has three guys and their hotshot Ellison. If we win this event, we win the meet. Understand?"

I nodded, feeling cold and clammy. "Sure, Coach."

"Cott's been running good, and ought to win this. He'll do four-ten or better. Rose might take second with a four-eleven or -twelve. But I'm worried about this kid Ellison. I don't like his stride. That kid can kill us."

I was glad to hear I wasn't the only one worrying about Bunny Ellison, the Culver bigfoot.

Coach continued, waving his sheet of curled up paper. "The only way we can win for sure is if we knock off Ellison. I don't figure you to win, any more than you do, right?"

"Well," I said.

"Okay," he said. "So you go out there and set the pace. Just like you did in practice last week. Ellison has to go after you. The crowd here won't let him play it safe. And by the time you've had it and drop out, Ellison will be running on an empty tank. Understand?"

"Right," I said. "And then Cott and Rose take him."

Coach's eyes gleamed. "You got it. Now get out there and fake out Ellison."

"What time do I need to do, Coach?" I said.

He smiled. "Make believe you're doing a four-minute mile. Hold it for three laps, and we'll take over for you. You got it?"

Hey, that's pretty funny, I told myself. Here you've been getting yourself all psyched up to win. And now you have to lose. How about that?

I didn't know if my old man was in the stands. But I knew Cindy was, and would be watching. Cheering.

For a rabbit? And I didn't have time to see her and explain.

My old man would understand, I thought. Coach gives the orders. You follow them. The school, the team comes first. That jazz.

I wondered if Mr. Robinson was here. The coach who ever dared to make him the rabbit would be out of a job for the rest of his life.

Well, you really didn't want to win anyway, right? I told myself. You didn't think you were good enough, and so on. You've been thinking of a million ways not to find out if you could win. So you wouldn't have to discover you were a rotten runner, after all.

Yeah, but that was before, I thought, angrily. Now it's different. I want to win, honest. I think I can win. I know it's crazy but . . . Hey, are you listening?

The gun went off. Maybe it scared me into a fast start. I had twenty yards on the field before the first short turn.

I tore up the first lap. Cott and Rose were well behind. I heard a big cheer. It wasn't for me. Bigfoot Ellison was coming up, his feet thudded into the ground like piledrivers.

Come on and catch me if you can, I said silently. I'm the rabbit.

The announcer called off the time. "Sixty seconds for the first quarter."

Right on the nose, I told myself. Three more like

that and you'll be a four-minute miler.

I tried to remember how I felt the time I beat Cott and Rose. I was flying then, not caring if I won or lost. Just out for the fun. Relaxed.

My body stretched out for the second lap. I was running so fast, I got scared. Save some, I told myself. You have to last three laps, remember. Don't burn out now.

I saw Ellison over my shoulder, about ten yards back. His face was tight and angry. His stride looked frightening. If I didn't go faster, he would run right over me.

Last turn of the second lap. Cott was close to Ellison, Rose just beyond him. The other Culver guys were strung out behind.

The announcer called off the time. "Time for the second lap, just under one minute. Davis of Emerson is now running one fifty-nine, under the all-city and all-state record."

I couldn't believe my ears. I was running only ten seconds over the best schoolboy time for the 800 meter—and doing it in a *mile*. What's happening? I wondered. Then I remembered my run with the ponytail girl, Julie Mars. I was fast that night, too. Why?

It's very simple, I told myself. You wanted to beat her, that's why.

Okay. So we'll do it again!

The third lap was going to be the killer. I had to carry the pace all the way through. Even improve on it, if possible, to give Cott some space for his finishing kick.

Somebody was at my shoulder. I looked up at Ellison. Go away, I wanted to say. I'm the rabbit nobody can catch.

I burned him on the first straightaway coming off the turn. Picked up five yards. Then he was thundering down the stretch after me. I hoped Cott and Rose wouldn't fall into any of the holes he was digging in the track.

Ellison caught me going around the last turn of the third lap. He didn't pass me but he was there. We were running shoulder to shoulder. The crowd was screaming. I hoped nobody would shoot me if I didn't turn over the lead.

I passed Coach. He had his hands cupped. "Okay, Davis. You can drop out any time."

I looked over my shoulder for Cott and Rose. And Ellison passed me.

The announcer called the time. "The last lap, one second over the minute. Davis is running at record mile time . . . and now it's Ellison of Culver taking the lead . . ."

I kept running. My side hurt, my chest hurt, my

neck and throat were burning with pain. You can't drop out, I told myself. Come on, run.

Rose went by me. He was laboring, gasping. Then Cott went by. I could swear I heard Cott breathing. I didn't think that was possible.

The stitch in my side didn't let me breathe. I lost my stride, fell off the pace.

Thirty yards ahead, Cott was closing on big Ellison. Rose was struggling, but he was still in third place. I heard steps behind me. The rest of the Culver team was closing the distance behind me.

I thought about Coach Gordon. Rotten fink! In the only race I ever wanted to win, he tells me I have to lose.

Hang on, I told myself. You'll get your second wind.

It came and I moved up. Then it was gone.

I got a third wind, and was working on the fourth. I understood what Cindy had told me about feeling as if her body was going to fall off.

My mind flashed a picture of Brogg in his box, the brain still alive, giving orders. You can do it, Brogg said.

We were on the long back stretch. Cott was on Ellison's heels, getting ready to jump him coming off the turn. Rose was falling back, I was flying again.

Rose, Cott, and Ellison, I thought suddenly.

There's my wheat, barley, and potatoes!

I pulled even with Rose. He stared at me with glazed, dead eyes. I went past him. *Sorry about that, Rose. This rabbit is still hopping.*

Cott was ten yards ahead. He'd pulled out and was running with Ellison. Ellison made his awesome stride longer. He went stride for stride with Cott. He wasn't fading, as Coach had thought he would. He wasn't running out of gas. He still had something left in his tank.

Brogg was beaming laser bullets into my skull. *You can do it you can do it you can do it.*

I couldn't blame Cott for looking sick when he saw me come up behind him. He was city champ, not me. I expected him to move over, let me pass. Instead, he stepped into my lane. Blocking me. Boxing me in behind him and Ellison.

My own team buddy! The enemy. Was pop right?

I was snarling. Breathing hard, gasping for air, and growling. *Rotten fink. I ran my heart out so you guys could win and now you try to hang me up and let me die!*

"I got the wheat. . . . You're the barley, Cott!"

I ran around him on the turn. The crowd was screaming. Now it was just me and the big horse Ellison, with sixty yards to go. Time for the finishing kick. I wasn't sure I had one.

My legs were dead when Brogg tuned in on me again. *You got the wheat and the barley. Now get the potatoes!*

A tidal wave of sound swept across the field. It was the crowd roaring. The din was deafening. I caught Ellison coming off the last curve. He looked sideways at me, his eyes rolling. I saw the fear there. I couldn't believe my old man could be right twice. It's okay, Ellison, I said silently, you're okay, I don't hate you, I just want this race.

He had been done in by the fast pace. He was finally out of gas, like me and everybody else. That awesome stride was shorter now. He was floundering all over the track. I passed Ellison in the last ten yards fighting for every inch. And then there was the tape waiting for me. Hey, I thought, that's the potatoes, not Ellison.

I ran through the tape. Coach was running alongside me yelling something in my ear. Go away, I wanted to say. I want to hear what Brogg says.

I heard him then. The pleased old voice from a planet away. *Well done, well done. Now you have your mountain!*

Cindy and I were at the movie again. *Brogg's Brain* revisited.

"You know," Cindy said, "this isn't such a dumb movie, after all."

"No, it isn't," I said. "No way is this a dumb movie."

"You may not believe this," Cindy said, "but while I was running my two-mile race, while you were in the john, I was very tired. I thought I would never finish, let alone win. And suddenly I heard Brogg talking to me."

"No kidding?" I said. "Hey, that's weird."

"Honest," Cindy said. "His voice kept bouncing around inside my head. He was saying, 'Come on, you can do it, you can do it, you can do it.' Would you believe it?"

"Well," I said, "to tell you the truth—"

A voice behind us growled. "Hey, would you kids mind shutting up? We came to see the movie."

I looked at Cindy. She nodded.

Hamburger time. Burrito time.

Time for a long talk on the long bus ride home.

About the Author

Kin Platt has written many outstanding novels for young adults, including *The Ape Inside Me,* and two books for younger readers, *Big Max* and *Big Max in the Mystery of the Missing Moose.* The author of the Max Roper mystery series for adults, Mr. Platt is also a noted cartoonist and former newspaperman. He lives in Los Angeles.

Platt, Kin.
    Brogg's brain.

        jW